# THE RESPIRATORY SYSTEM

Words in *italic* in the main
text (*or in* Roman *type in
the captions*) are explained
in the Index and glossary at
the end of the book.

A Cherrytree Book

Adapted by A S Publishing
from *APARATO RESPIRATORIO
SOPLO DE VIDA*
by Núria Roca and Marta Serrano
illustrated by Antonio Muñoz Tenllado
designed by Rosa Mª Moreno
produced by Rafael Marfil
© Parramón Ediciones, S.A. 1995

This edition first published 1996
by Cherrytree Press Ltd
Windsor Bridge Road
Bath, Avon BA2 3AX

© Cherrytree Press Ltd 1996

British Library Cataloguing in Publication Data

The respiratory system. – (Invisible world)
 1. Respiratory organs – Juvenile literature  2. Respiratory
 organs – Anatomy – Juvenile literature
 I. Halton, Frances
 611.2

ISBN 0-7451-5282-1

Typeset by Dorchester Typesetting Group Ltd. Dorset
Printed in Spain

# THE RESPIRATORY
# SYSTEM

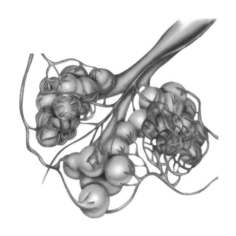

Edited by
Frances Halton

CHERRYTREE BOOKS

# The breath of life

We need *oxygen* to live. This gas is used by our cells to break down, or 'burn', our food and give us energy. We get our oxygen from the air around us. This contains 21 per cent of oxygen and 78 per cent of *nitrogen*, together with small amounts of *carbon dioxide* and other gases.

Air comes into our bodies through our *lungs*, when we breathe in. Oxygen from the air is transferred to our blood, which carries it round to all the cells in our body. In the cells the oxygen from the blood is used to 'burn' our food, and the gas carbon dioxide is produced and carried away by the blood. The carbon dioxide is carried back to the lungs, from which it can be breathed out of the body.

The whole process is called respiration. It has three phases. *External respiration* is breathing in and out, and the exchange of oxygen and carbon dioxide in the lungs. *Internal transport* is the carriage of oxygen and carbon dioxide in the blood between the lungs and the cells. *Cellular*, or *internal*, *respiration* is the use of oxygen and the production of carbon dioxide in the cells.

The respiratory system is a channel that begins at the nose and continues through the *throat* and the windpipe, or *trachea*. The windpipe divides into two tubes, called *bronchi*, that lead to the two lungs. In the lungs, the bronchi split into lots of tiny branches called *bronchioles*. The bronchioles lead to millions of tiny air-sacs called *alveoli*.

The respiratory system is closely linked to the *circulatory system*, or blood system. Blood which has picked up a supply of oxygen in the lungs goes to the left side· of the *heart* and is then pumped round the body to take oxygen to every cell. Stale blood carrying carbon dioxide from the cells goes back to the right side of the heart, from where it is pumped to the lungs. There it releases its carbon dioxide and picks up more oxygen before starting another circuit of the body.

*The amount of oxygen in the atmosphere varies; it gets less with altitude. As we climb higher, we need to breathe in more air to provide the blood with its normal amount of oxygen. Climbers often suffer from altitude sickness. These are some of the symptoms they suffer.* ▼

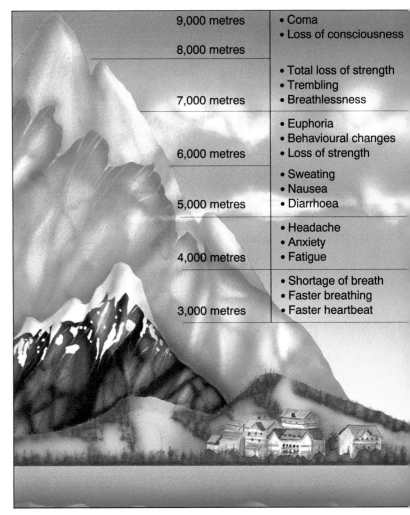

| 9,000 metres | • Coma |
| 8,000 metres | • Loss of consciousness |
| 7,000 metres | • Total loss of strength<br>• Trembling<br>• Breathlessness |
| 6,000 metres | • Euphoria<br>• Behavioural changes<br>• Loss of strength |
| 5,000 metres | • Sweating<br>• Nausea<br>• Diarrhoea |
| 4,000 metres | • Headache<br>• Anxiety<br>• Fatigue |
| 3,000 metres | • Shortage of breath<br>• Faster breathing<br>• Faster heartbeat |

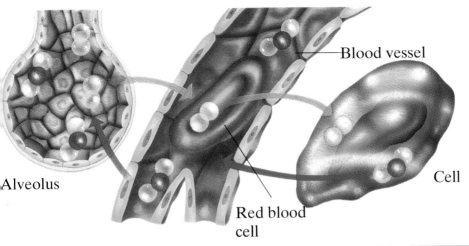

Blood vessel

Alveolus

Cell

Red blood cell

◀ *External respiration (left) supplies oxygen ($O_2$) to the blood in the alveoli. In internal respiration (right) the cells use the oxygen to release energy. Carbon dioxide ($CO_2$) is produced as a waste product.*

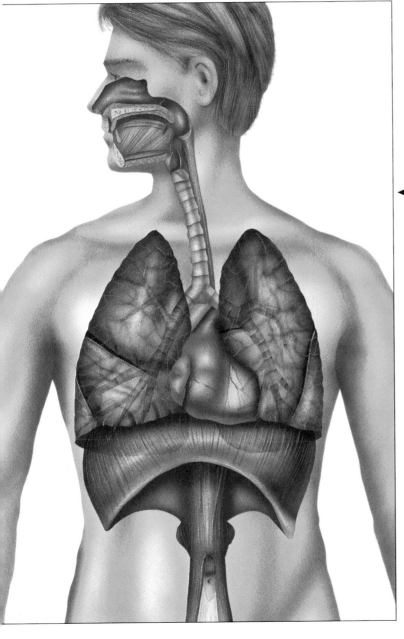

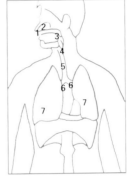

NITROGEN 78%

OXYGEN 21%

CARBON DIOXIDE

ARGON AND OTHER GASES

◀ *In the nose, each* nostril (**1**) *opens into the nasal cavity (**2**). This leads to the* pharynx (**3**) *which connects with the mouth cavity and the* larynx (**4**), *in which lie the* vocal cords. *The pharynx and larynx together make up the throat. Next comes the trachea (**5**) which forks into two bronchi (**6**). These enter the lungs (**7**), where they subdivide into bronchioles, leading finally to alveoli.*

▲

*The air around us is made up of a mixture of gases, most of it nitrogen which the body does not use. The air also contains water vapour, the amount of which varies with the humidity of the atmosphere.*

# Air conditioning

The air we breathe contains many impurities, such as particles of dust, pollen, fungus spores and bacteria. Sometimes it is very cold, and sometimes very dry. If it reached our lungs like this, it could cause infections and other problems. So, as it travels down the passages of the respiratory system, it is 'conditioned' by being moistened, warmed and filtered.

As the air passes through the upper respiratory passages, it picks up moisture from the *mucus* produced by the *mucous membrane* that lines them. As a result, it will not dry out the lower passages of the respiratory system. The membrane has many blood vessels close to its surface and so the air is warmed up to 37°C, the temperature of blood. Sometimes, on a very dry and cold day, the system cannot cope and the cold, dry air rasps your air passages as you breathe in.

Many particles are trapped by hairs in the nostrils, and more by the mucus in the *nasal passages*. The film of mucus with these particles is moved towards the throat by tiny hairlike *cilia*, which project from the mucous membrane. When the mucus reaches the throat, it is expelled from the body by coughing, or it may be swallowed.

At the back of the nasal passages and the throat are the *adenoids* and *tonsils*, clumps of *lymph tissue* that trap and destroy bacteria.

By the time the air reaches our lungs it should be damp, warm and practically free from particles. But if we breathe through the mouth, none of these processes is carried out really efficiently. This is why it is better to breathe through the nose.

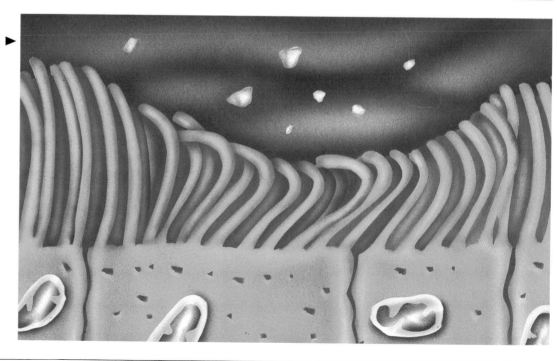

*The mucous membranes are covered with hairlike projections called cilia (**1**) which wave about constantly. They move along a film of mucus (**2**) in which impurities are trapped (**3**); this mucus can then be swallowed or coughed, sneezed or spat out.*

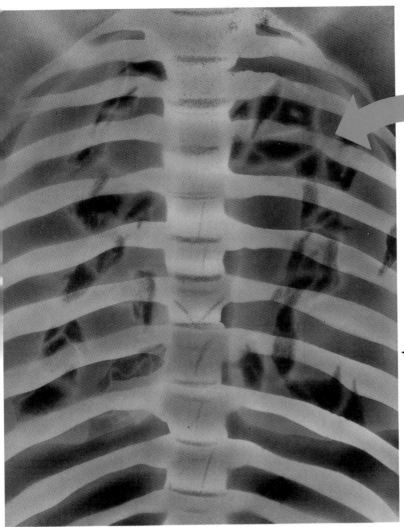

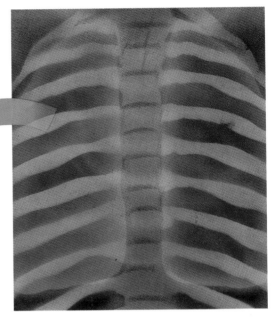

◀ *The defence mechanisms of the respiratory system are usually able to trap and expel particles of foreign substances, such as silica dust. But when a great deal of dust is breathed in, they may not be able to filter it all out. Deposits of silica may build up in the lungs, causing the illness called silicosis that used to be common among miners. This prevents efficient breathing. The X-ray above shows healthy lungs; that on the left shows the shadows formed by the silica.*

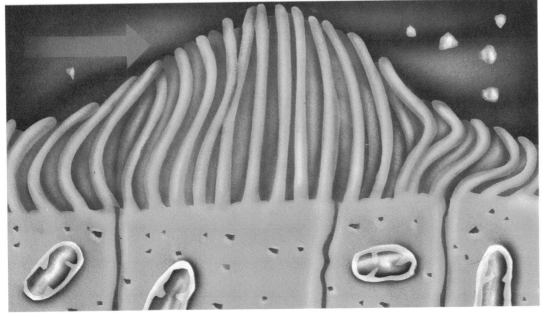

# Breathing in

Air enters our body mainly through the nose. We can also breathe through the mouth but, as we have seen, the air does not reach our lungs in such good condition if we do so.

The nose is a roughly pyramid-shaped structure of bone and *cartilage* in the centre of the face. At its base are two openings called nostrils, separated from each other by a wall of cartilage and bone called the nasal septum.

Each nostril opens into a nasal cavity through an entrance called the vestibulum, which is lined with stiff hairs designed to trap particles in the air. Almost all of the nasal cavity is lined with a thin mucous membrane with a plentiful blood supply, and covered with cilia. On the roof of each nasal cavity is a patch of a different kind of mucous membrane, in which are *receptor cells* sensitive to smell. If you have a bad cold, these may become covered by thick mucus and until this clears up you lose your sense of smell.

At the back of the nose the nasal cavities lead into the pharynx, the upper part of the throat. They are also connected with hollow spaces in the skull bones, called *sinuses*, lined with mucous membrane. These simply serve to make the skull lighter and play no part in breathing.

Sometimes the nasal cavities are irritated by particles breathed in. This makes you sneeze. The particles stimulate the sensitive cells of the nasal mucous membrane. This sends an impulse to the *central nervous system*, which triggers off the contraction of some of the respiratory muscles. Air is breathed in deeply and then forced out sharply through the nose again, with luck taking the irritating particles with it. Sneezing happens without our conscious control.

*A sneeze has four stages: we take in a deep breath (**1**); the glottis in the larynx opens completely (**2**); the soft palate is lowered (**3**); and air is forced out of our lungs and through our air passages very sharply (**4**), often sweeping the irritating substance away with it.*
▼

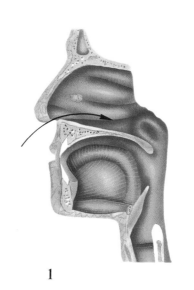

1

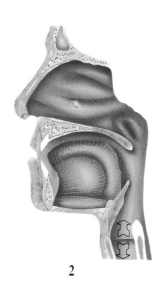

3

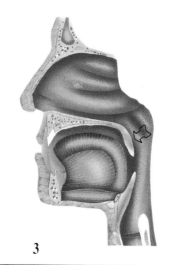

2

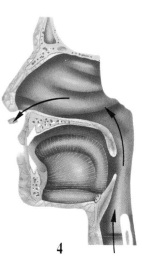

4

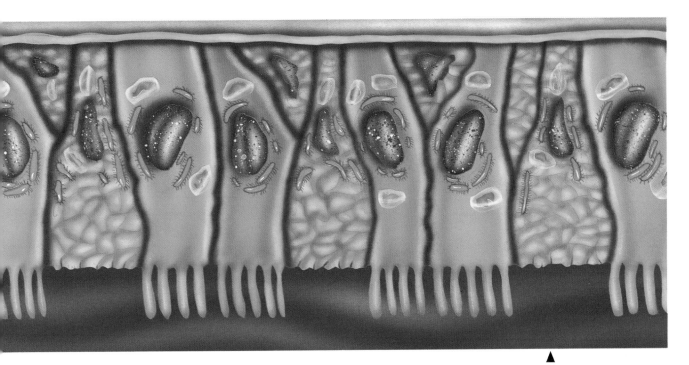

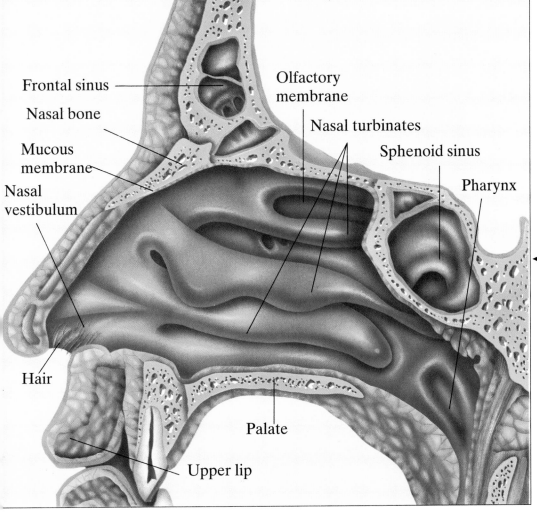

Frontal sinus

Nasal bone

Mucous
membrane

Nasal
vestibulum

Hair

Olfactory
membrane

Nasal turbinates

Sphenoid sinus

Pharynx

Palate

Upper lip

*The cells lining the respiratory passages produce lots of sticky mucus. Dust particles trapped in this are wafted along by the hairlike cilia and prevented from entering the lungs.*

◄ *Air is warmed and moistened as it flows over the folded surfaces of the nasal turbinates. The olfactory membrane contains smell receptors linked to the brain. The sinuses are cavities in the skull linked to the nose.*

# The throat

We breathe air in through the nasal passages and into the throat. This is made up of two parts, the pharynx and the larynx.

The pharynx is a tube about 12 to 14 centimetres long that runs down in front of the vertebral column, narrowing as it goes. The upper part of the pharynx also connects with two structures, known as the Eustachian tubes, which lead to the ears.

The middle section of the pharynx opens into the back of the mouth, allowing us to breathe through the mouth. Although it is not as good as breathing through the nose, it is very useful if your nose is blocked by a heavy cold. The lower part of the pharynx leads into the larynx and also into the food passage called the *oesophagus* (gullet).

The larynx is shaped like an upside-down cone, about 3 to 4 centimetres long. It is made up of nine cartilages and many small muscles. At its entrance is a flap of cartilage called the *epiglottis*.

The larynx is also called the voice box, because it contains our vocal cords. These are made of stretchy fibrous tissue and we use them to speak. The space between the vocal cords is called the glottis. The inside of the larynx is covered with mucous membrane. The lower end of the larynx leads into the trachea.

It is very important that food should not get into the respiratory passages and block off the air supply. To prevent this, the larynx is sealed off from the pharynx when we swallow. The larynx moves upwards and forwards, placing itself underneath the base of the *tongue*. The epiglottis moves across the top of the larynx and blocks it off, while the muscles of the vocal cords contract, closing the glottis. As a result, food is pushed towards the oesophagus and down the digestive tract. After we have swallowed, the air passages can safely open up again.

Sometimes food or liquid does get into the larynx and we choke. We may be able to cough the obstruction out, or a sharp thump on the back or squeeze of the *chest* may help to push air out of our lungs with enough force to carry the obstruction away with it.

*The larynx is made up of strips of cartilage joined to one another by membranes and ligaments. The larynx makes a bulge in the lower part of the neck. Because the larynx is larger and sticks out more in men than in women, this bulge is known as the Adam's apple.*
▼

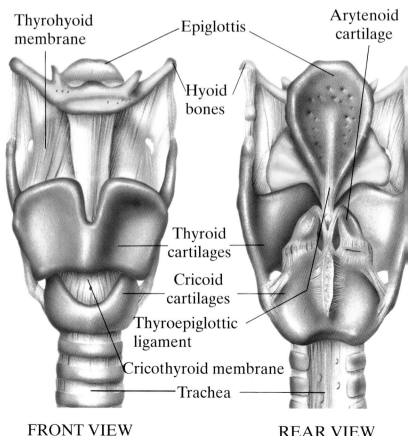

Thyrohyoid membrane

Epiglottis

Arytenoid cartilage

Hyoid bones

Thyroid cartilages

Cricoid cartilages

Thyroepiglottic ligament

Cricothyroid membrane

Trachea

FRONT VIEW

REAR VIEW

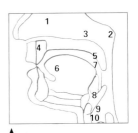

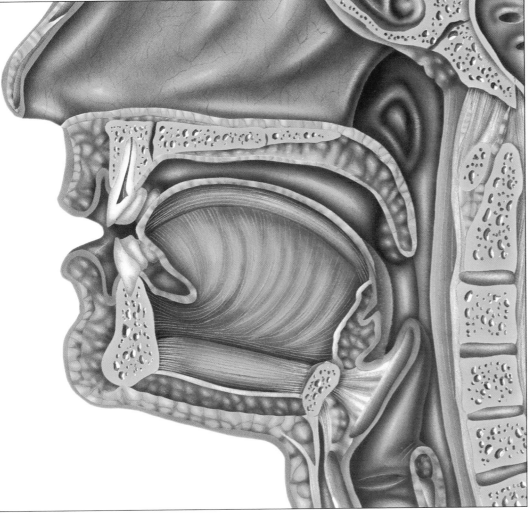

*This section through the face and neck shows the pharynx and how it connects with the cavities of the nose and mouth, and with the larynx: nasal septum (**1**), adenoid (**2**), palate (**3**), upper jawbone (**4**), soft palate (**5**), tongue (**6**), tonsil (**7**), epiglottis (**8**), larynx (**9**), vocal cords (**10**).*

*Both the respiratory system and digestive system lead off the mouth cavity, and a clever mechanism prevents food entering the respiratory tract. When we want to swallow, the larynx moves upwards and forwards, under the tongue, and the epiglottis moves to block off the larynx. The soft palate moves across to block the nasal cavity. The food can pass safely down the digestive tract and the larynx quickly opens to take in air again.*

▼

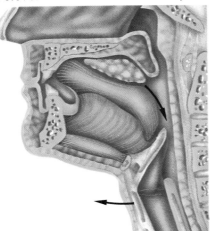
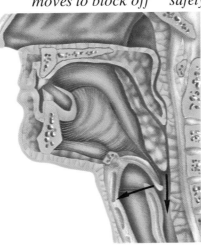
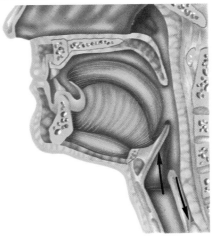

# How we speak

The air we take into our bodies not only brings lifegiving oxygen; it also allows us to speak. We do this through structures that alter the flow of air from the lungs and others that act as *resonance chambers*.

Most of the time the vocal cords in the larynx lie apart and the air passes freely through the V-shaped space between them, the glottis, without disturbing them. When we want to speak, we can contract the vocal cords and draw them together. Then air brushing against them makes them vibrate. The sounds produced by the vibration are the voice.

The sounds produced by the vocal cords depend on their length and tension, which alter the frequency of the vibrations. The shorter and tighter the cords, the higher-pitched the sound; the longer and more relaxed, the deeper the voice. The vocal cords of an adult man are between 20 and 35 millimetres long, while those of adult women and children are between 15 and 20 millimetres. This is why men have deeper voices.

The loudness of the sounds we make depends on the volume and speed of the air we push out from the lungs through the vocal cords. A lot of air makes a loud noise, while a whisper needs only a tiny breath.

The quality of the sounds we make is also affected by the shape of the body's resonance chambers. These are the hollow spaces in the head through which the air passes, including the mouth cavity, the pharynx, and the nasal passages.

The sinuses in the skull and to some extent the chest cavity also act as resonators. The different size and shape of these in each person gives their voice its own individual sound.

Air passing through the vocal cords makes simple sounds or notes; these are turned into speech, or articulated, by the way in which we position the pharynx, mouth, and tongue as the sound passes through.

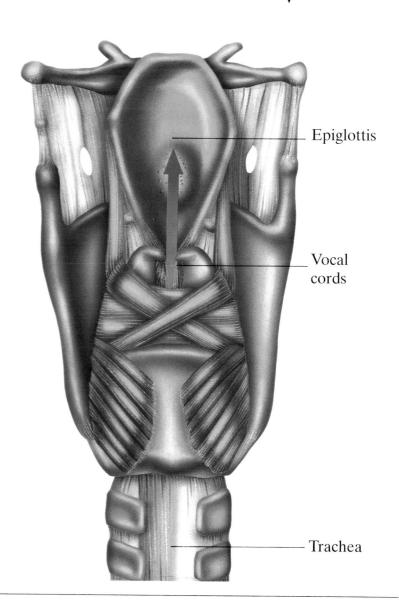

*The larynx from the back. You can see how air is breathed out through the glottis, the space between the vocal cords.*

▼

Epiglottis

Vocal cords

Trachea

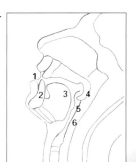

*The characteristic ▶ sound of your voice comes from the resonance of air as it passes out of your mouth. This is affected by the shape of your lips (**1**), teeth (**2**), tongue (**3**), soft palate (**4**), pharynx (**5**) and larynx (**6**), your cheeks, your sinuses and even your chest.*

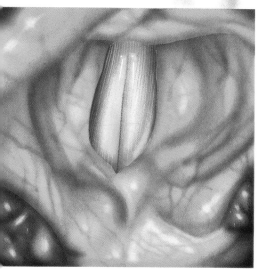

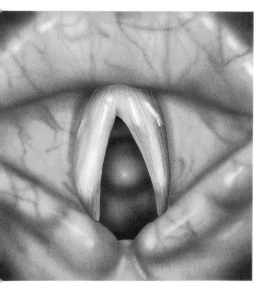

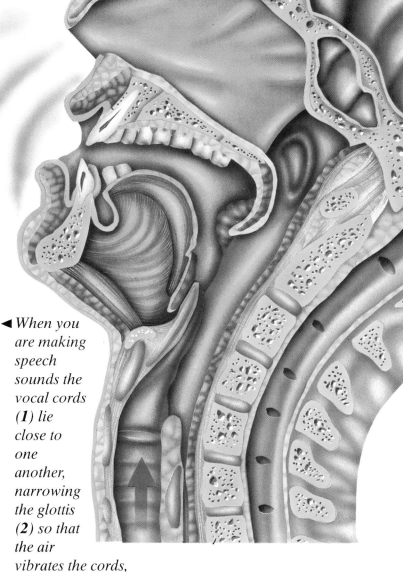

*◀ When you are making speech sounds the vocal cords (**1**) lie close to one another, narrowing the glottis (**2**) so that the air vibrates the cords, causing a sound. When they are at rest, the vocal cords (**3**) lie against the walls of the larynx and the triangular opening of the glottis (**4**) allows air to flow through soundlessly.*

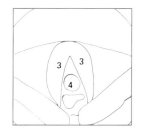

# Passage to the lungs

The larynx leads to the trachea, a tube about 12 centimetres long and 2.5 centimetres wide, which goes down the neck and into the chest, or thorax. It runs in front of the oesophagus. The trachea is fairly rigid since its walls are made up of a series of C-shaped open rings of cartilage. At the back of the trachea are smoooth muscle fibres, which can alter the diameter of the tube, and inside is a lining of mucous membrane.

At its lower end, in the chest behind the *breastbone*, or sternum, the trachea divides into two bronchi. These lead into the two lungs. Inside the lungs the bronchi divide again and again to form a branching structure known as the *bronchial tree*, made up of a number of smaller and smaller bronchioles. The larger 'branches' have rings of cartilage in their walls; the smaller branches are made of stretchy muscle tissue. The bronchioles lead to alveoli, tiny air sacs which look rather like clusters of grapes.

If irritating substances get as far as the larynx, trachea and bronchi we cough. After a deep breath our lungs contract to force breath out at high speed, taking with it the irritating substance. We also cough when our air passages are infected and produce a thick, sticky mucus called phlegm. We often cough when we have a cold, and this is not serious, but a long-lasting or painful cough should be treated by a doctor.

*A cough may be an involuntary reflex action or may be deliberate. When we cough, we take in a deep breath (1) and close the glottis (2). The respiratory muscles contract (3), and suddenly the vocal cords open and air is forced out under pressure at high speed (4) to push the irritating substance out with it. We also cough to bring up thick mucus from the air passages when they are infected.*

▼

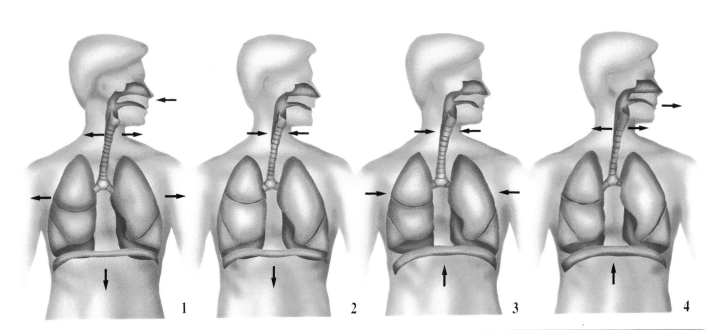

1    2    3    4

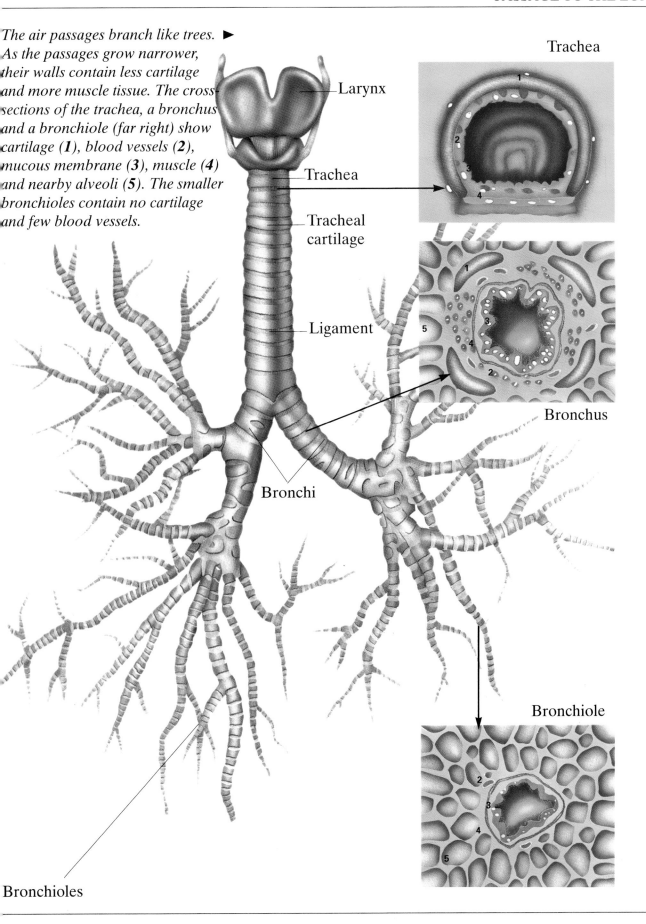

*The air passages branch like trees.* ▶
*As the passages grow narrower,
their walls contain less cartilage
and more muscle tissue. The cross-
sections of the trachea, a bronchus
and a bronchiole (far right) show
cartilage (1), blood vessels (2),
mucous membrane (3), muscle (4)
and nearby alveoli (5). The smaller
bronchioles contain no cartilage
and few blood vessels.*

Larynx

Trachea

Tracheal
cartilage

Ligament

Bronchi

Bronchioles

Trachea

Bronchus

Bronchiole

# The lungs

In our lungs oxygen from the air is absorbed into the blood, and carbon dioxide is removed from the blood so that it can be breathed out. The lungs lie in the thoracic cavity, the hollow chamber inside the chest which is surrounded and protected by the ribs, the spine and the breastbone. The chest cavity is separated from the *abdomen* by a dome-shaped sheet of muscle called the *diaphragm*. The lungs take up almost all of the chest cavity; the left lung is a little smaller than the right, since part of the chest cavity on that side is taken up by the heart. On the outer surface of the lungs are grooves that divide them into lobes, three in the right lung and two in the left.

The inside of the lung is rather like a sponge, with a network of branching air passages leading to clusters of alveoli, called alveolar sacs. These are full of air and have very thin walls, the inner surface of which is covered with a film of water. The alveoli also contain cells called *macrophages*, which surround and destroy germs and other particles which have escaped the filters in the air passages. Each lung contains about 300 million alveoli; together they have a surface area of about 70 square metres.

The alveoli are surrounded by a network of tiny blood vessels called *capillaries*, so that each looks rather like a ball in a string bag. The capillaries also have very thin walls, so only half a thousandth of a millimetre separates the air from the blood.

Each lung is surrounded by a stretchy double membrane called a *pleura*. The inner layer of the pleura is wrapped round the lung, and the outer layer lines the inside of the chest cavity and is attached to the chest walls. The space between the two layers contains a small amount of liquid which allows the two layers to slide over one another.

*The lungs are protected by the ribs, spine and breastbone. The right lung has three lobes, the left only two. This is because the heart also lies in the left side of the chest cavity.*
▼

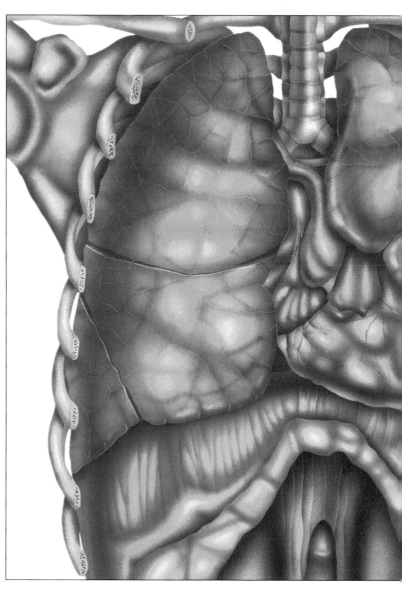

The space between the alveoli and the capillaries surrounding them is so slight that the exchange of gases between them is easy. This illustration shows a section through a complete alveolus and parts of four others (*1*). Between them lies supportive connective tissue (*2*). The walls of the alveoli (*3*) contain several kinds of cells (*4* and *5*) and are lined with a very thin film of water. A macrophage (*6*) fights infection and two capillaries (*7*) collect and deliver blood.

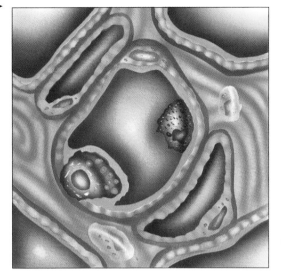

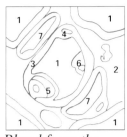

*Blood from the body, high in carbon dioxide, is carried to the lungs by the pulmonary artery. Carbon dioxide diffuses into the alveoli from the capillaries. Oxygen from breathed-in air diffuses into the capillaries and is carried to the pulmonary vein which goes to the heart.*

▲
*The lungs are surrounded by a double membrane called the pleura (shown in blue).*

Bronchiole

Branch of pulmonary vein

Branch of pulmonary artery

Alveolus

# How we breathe

There are two stages to our breathing: *inhalation*, or inspiration, when we draw air into the lungs, and *exhalation*, or expiration, when we breathe out. These stages are controlled by muscles that alter the pressure within the lungs when they contract or relax. The muscles are controlled by the *nervous system*.

Inhalation happens when the space inside the chest cavity increases. Air then rushes into the lungs and expands them. The main muscles involved in inhalation are the diaphragm and the external intercostals between the ribs.

When the diaphragm contracts it flattens and moves downwards, increasing the size of the chest cavity from top to bottom. When the external intercostal muscles contract, they lift the lower ribs outwards and push the breastbone forwards, increasing the size of the chest cavity from front to back. Other muscles help to increase the size of the chest when we need to take an extra deep breath, or are having difficulty breathing.

When we have finished breathing in, our muscles relax. The chest cavity becomes smaller again, and this squeezes the lungs so that air is forced out of them. If we want to breathe out very hard, we use the internal intercostal muscles to pull the ribs quickly downwards and the abdominal muscles to pull the diaphragm upwards.

*When we breathe in, the diaphragm is lowered and this enlarges the chest cavity from top to bottom. At the same time the external intercostal muscles lift the ribs, again enlarging the chest cavity. When we breathe out, the chest cavity becomes smaller as the diaphragm rises and the ribs sink.* ▼

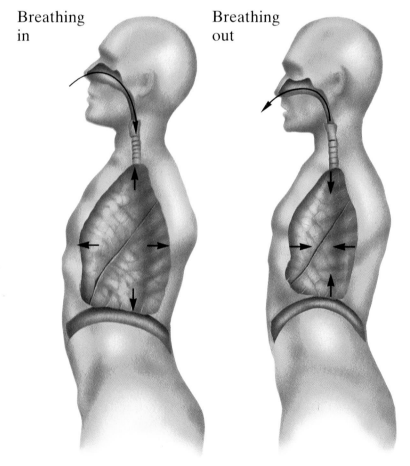

Breathing in

Breathing out

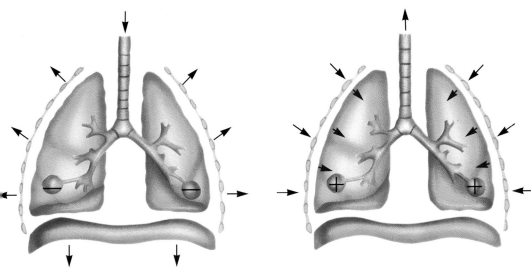

◄ When we breathe in, the chest expands and air is sucked into the lungs to fill the space. When we breathe out, the chest cavity becomes smaller and pressure on the alveoli forces air out of the lungs.

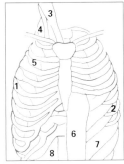

◄ When we breathe in normally, we use the external intercostal muscles (**1**) to lift the ribs and expand the chest. When breathing deeply, we also use other muscles in the chest and neck (**2**, **3** and **4**). When we breathe out strongly, we use the internal intercostals (**5**) and other muscles (**6** and **7**) in the chest and abdomen. The diaphragm (**8**) is used in all breathing movements.

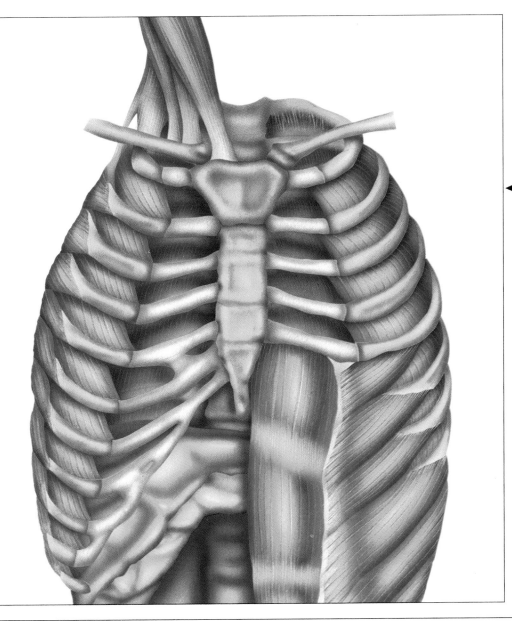

# How much breath?

When we are sitting quietly or resting, our bodies do not need a great deal of oxygen and we breathe quietly, around 12 times a minute. Most of the time we are not even aware that we are breathing. But when we are running around or making any other sort of physical effort we use up a lot of oxygen. Our breathing speeds up so that more oxygen is drawn into our lungs, from which it can quickly be carried round the body in the bloodstream.

Under normal conditions of light activity an adult male breathes about 500 millilitres (0.5 litres) of air in and out in each respiratory cycle. This is known as the *tidal air*. By taking deep breaths you can take in an extra quantity of air – about 3 litres for a man and 2 litres for a woman. This is called the *inhalatory reserve volume*.

When you breathe out normally, a lot of air remains in your lungs, so there is still plenty of oxygen for the blood to pick up between breaths. If you breathe out as hard as you can, you get rid of the *exhalatory reserve volume*; it is about 1 litre for men and 700 millilitres for women.

Even after you breathe out all the air you possibly can, some still remains in the lungs – about 1,200 millilitres in a man and 1,100 millilitres in a woman. This is called the *residual volume*. It is only forced out when the lung loses its elasticity and collapses. This can happen when air gets into the space between the two layers of the pleura, for example after a chest injury in which a broken rib tears through the pleura.

Only about 350 millilitres of each normal breath actually reaches the alveoli to be used in the exchange of gases. About 150 millilitres of air remains permanently in the alveoli, in what is called the *dead air space*.

The *vital air capacity* equals all the air you can breathe in and out of your lungs, taking the deepest possible breaths. It is roughly 5 litres.

*A certain amount of air, known as the residual volume, always remains in the lungs even after breathing out as deeply as possible. Apart from this, the amount of air in the lungs depends whether we are breathing normally or taking deliberately deep breaths.* ▶

*The amount of air ▶ in the lungs at any time depends on how strongly we are breathing. It can also vary with age, sex and health, so the figures given here are only approximate.*

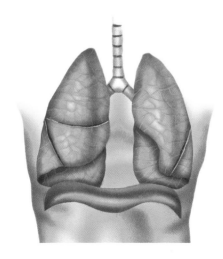

Air breathed in and out at rest: 500 ml

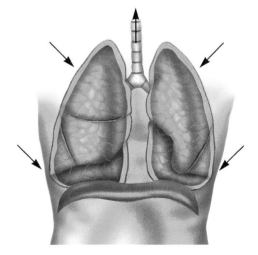

Air expelled in forced breath: 500 ml + 1,000 ml

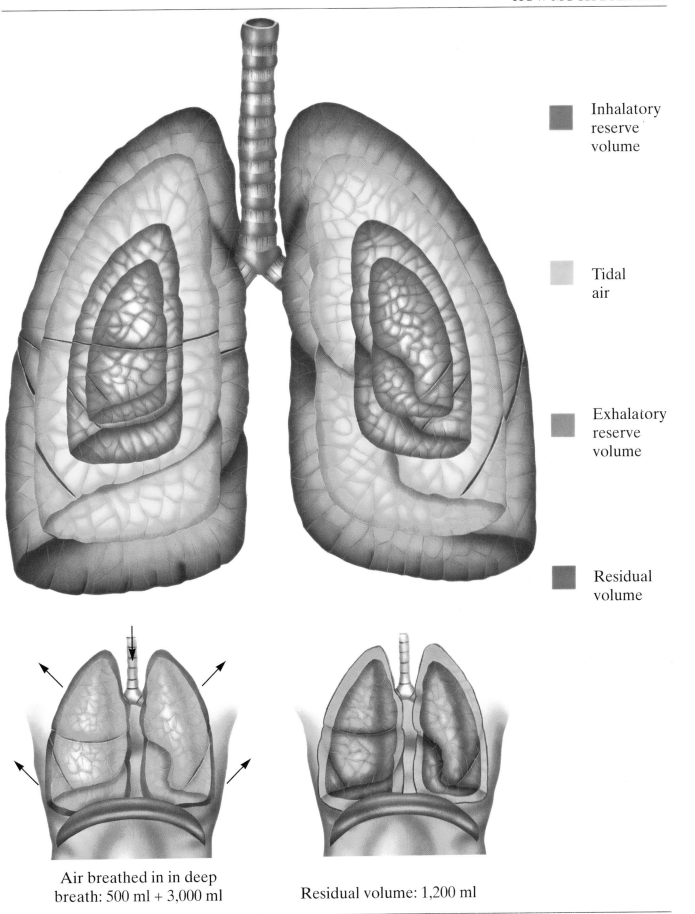

Inhalatory
reserve
volume

Tidal
air

Exhalatory
reserve
volume

Residual
volume

Air breathed in in deep
breath: 500 ml + 3,000 ml

Residual volume: 1,200 ml

# Exchange of gases

The air that we breathe into the alveoli is rich in oxygen. In contrast the blood that is pumped from the right side of the heart into the lungs has given up its oxygen to the body cells; instead it is carrying the waste product carbon dioxide, produced during cellular respiration. The walls of the alveoli and the surrounding capillaries are so thin that it is possible for the oxygen and carbon dioxide to be exchanged, or diffused, between them, with oxygen from the air in the lungs passing to the blood and carbon dioxide moving in the other direction.

The carbon dioxide from the blood passes through the walls of the capillary, across a minute space and through the wall of the alveolus into the film of moisture that lines it. Meanwhile oxygen from the air dissolves in this moist layer before moving through the alveolar wall and into the capillary. There it locks on to the red cells in the blood.

The surface area of the alveoli, and so the area involved in this interchange, is very large. The capillaries are so narrow that the red blood cells brush against their walls as they squeeze through, and this makes it easier for the gases to diffuse. There is time for substances to be exhanged through the capillary walls because although blood flows very quickly through arteries and veins, it moves only slowly through the tiny capillaries. Even so, the exchange of gases takes place in less than a second.

At the end of the capillary network the tiny vessels merge to form veins which take the freshly oxygenated blood to the left side of the heart. From there it is pumped through *arteries* and smaller blood vessels to all the body's cells, taking its load of oxygen with it. The carbon dioxide which the alveoli now contain is breathed out, together with a little water vapour from the moist lining of the alveoli. We can see this moisture as a little cloud when we breathe out on a cold day.

*Blood from the heart (shown in blue) is laden with carbon dioxide. In life it is dark red. As it passes the alveolus it sheds its carbon dioxide and picks up oxygen. The oxygenated blood (shown in red) now looks bright red. It flows back to the heart, from which it will be pumped around the body.*

▼

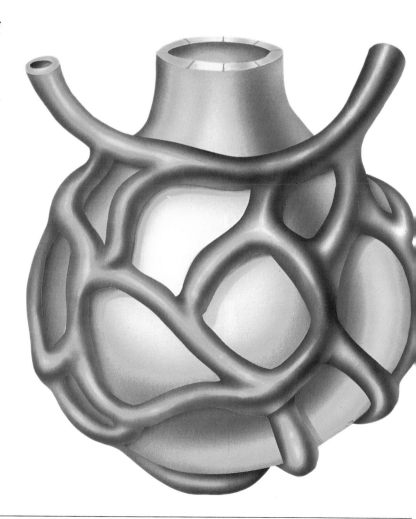

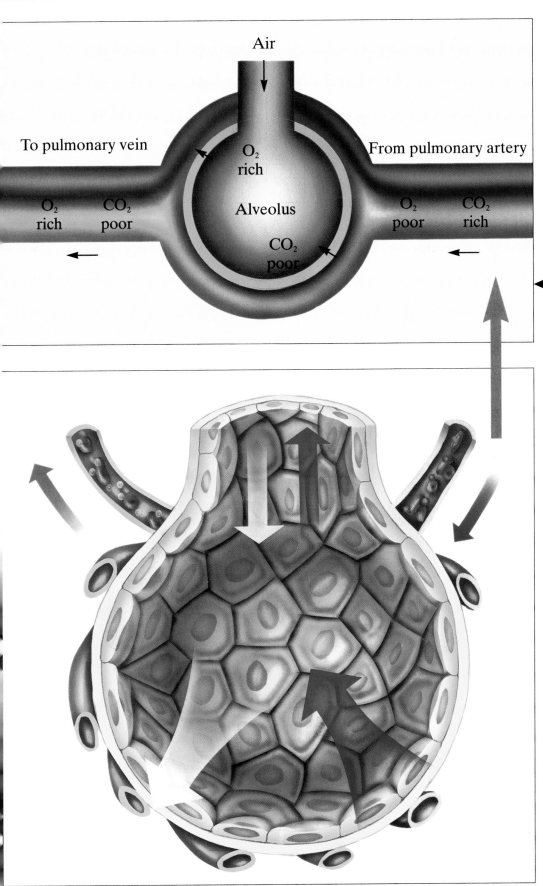

Air

To pulmonary vein

O$_2$ rich

Alveolus

From pulmonary artery

O$_2$ rich

CO$_2$ poor

CO$_2$ poor

O$_2$ poor

CO$_2$ rich

*Capillaries from the pulmonary arteries bring blood to the alveolus that is low in oxygen (O$_2$) and rich in carbon dioxide (CO$_2$). This venous blood (**1**) releases CO$_2$ (**2**) into the alveolus so that it can be breathed out of the body. Meanwhile O$_2$ (**3**) from the air in the alveolus enters the capillaries. They take the freshly oxygenated blood (**4**) to the pulmonary veins which carry it to the heart.*

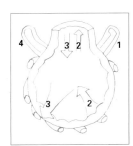

# Round the body

The oxygen we breathe in is carried round the body by the blood. The red cells in the blood contain molecules of a substance called *haemoglobin*, which contains iron. Oxygen locks on to the haemoglobin and is carried round to the cells. When it reaches a cell that is short of oxygen, the haemoglobin releases its load across the thin cell wall. Within the cell, the process of cellular respiration takes place. The cell uses the oxygen to 'burn' food, in the form of glucose, to produce energy. The chemical reaction that takes place releases waste carbon dioxide and water. The carbon dioxide is taken up by the blood *plasma* and returned to the lungs to be breathed out.

The heart pumps blood through two separate circuits of the circulatory system. The left chamber of the heart contains blood rich in oxygen, carried on the haemoglobin molecules of its red cells. The beating of the heart pumps the blood out through the large arteries and smaller blood vessels into all the organs and tissues of the body except the lungs. The tissues take up from the blood the oxygen they need as fuel, and in exchange the waste product carbon dioxide passes into the blood. The blood continues its journey through the *veins* into the right chamber of the heart. At this stage the blood is dark red in colour. This journey is known as the systemic circulation.

From the right side of the heart, blood is pumped through the pulmonary arteries into the lungs. The carbon dioxide from the blood passes into the alveoli while the oxygen from the air moves across to the blood. This freshly oxygenated blood, bright red in colour, now travels to the left side of the heart, from which the cycle begins all over again. The circuit from the heart to the lungs and back is known as the pulmonary circulation.

*The pulmonary veins take freshly oxygenated blood from the lungs to the left side of the heart. From there it is pumped through arteries and* arterioles *to all parts of the body. In the fine capillaries, it releases oxygen and picks up carbon dioxide. It then travels back through the veins to the right side of the heart. From there it is pumped along the pulmonary arteries to the lungs, where it sheds its carbon dioxide and picks up a fresh supply of oxygen.*

*The red blood cells contain the pigment haemoglobin, which gives them their red colour. Each molecule of haemoglobin is made up of chains of amino acids, linked to molecules of iron-containing heme (shown as red discs). Haemoglobin readily picks up oxygen from the lungs and then becomes bright red. It releases oxygen when it reaches the cells and becomes dark red again.* ▶

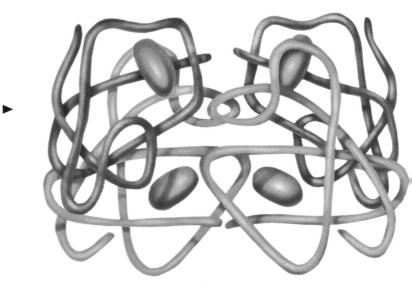

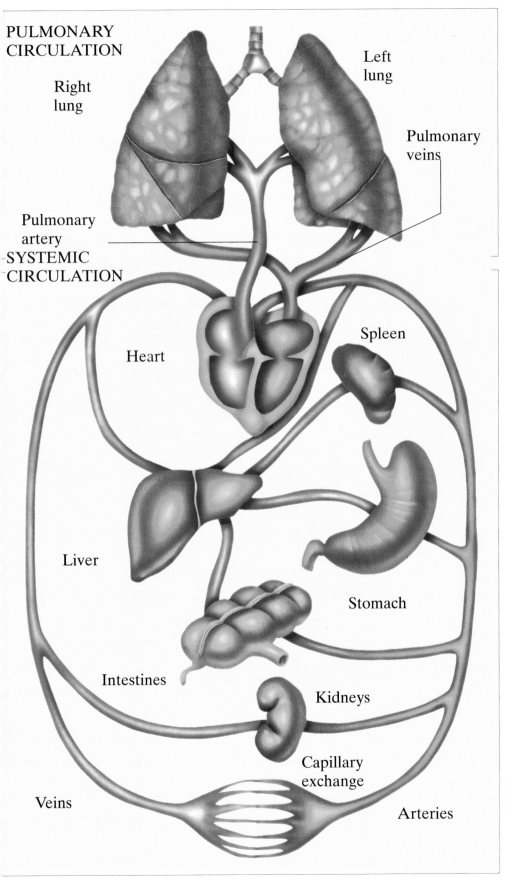

**PULMONARY CIRCULATION**

Right lung

Left lung

Pulmonary veins

Pulmonary artery

**SYSTEMIC CIRCULATION**

Heart

Spleen

Liver

Stomach

Intestines

Kidneys

Capillary exchange

Veins

Arteries

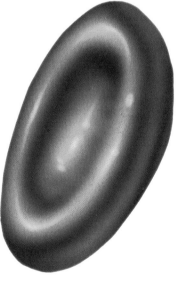

*The red blood cells are responsible for carrying oxygen. They are shaped like flattened discs, and contain the red pigment haemoglobin. One cubic centimetre of blood may contain 5,500 million of them.*
▼

# Controlling our breathing

Supplying oxygen to our cells and removing the waste carbon dioxide is so vital that it must be very carefully controlled. This is done by the *respiratory centre* in the *medulla oblongata* of the *brain*. This regulates the activity of the respiratory muscles so that the right amount of air is breathed in to suit whatever activity we are carrying out.

The respiratory centre is made up of two groups of *neurons* (nerve cells) that work alternately, one controlling breathing in and one controlling breathing out. This area allows us to alter the rate at which we breathe when we want to, since it is connected to the *cerebral cortex* of the brain which regulates voluntary movements (those made by our conscious decisions). But we cannot stop ourselves breathing altogether, as the respiratory centre will then override the cerebral cortex and take control of our breathing.

The activity of the respiratory centre is regulated by nerve endings called *chemoreceptors* in the *aorta* and carotid arteries. These are sensitive to the chemical composition of the blood. When they detect that the amount of carbon dioxide in the blood is high, for example when the body is using up oxygen quickly during exercise, the chemoreceptors send nerve stimuli to the respiratory centre, which makes us breathe faster. More air – and so more oxygen – enters the lungs. The heart beats faster to send the oxygenated blood round the body more quickly, so that it can remove the excess carbon dioxide. When exercise stops and the cells produce less carbon dioxide, the rate of breathing and the heart beat slow down.

Respiration is also regulated by *stretch receptors*. When the lungs enlarge as we breathe in they pull these receptors, and at a certain tension they send nerve impulses to the respiratory centre so that we stop breathing in.

*Most of the time we breathe withou* *being aware of what we are doing. Stretch receptors detect the increase in the volume of our lungs as we breathe in. When they reach a certain tension they send a signal*

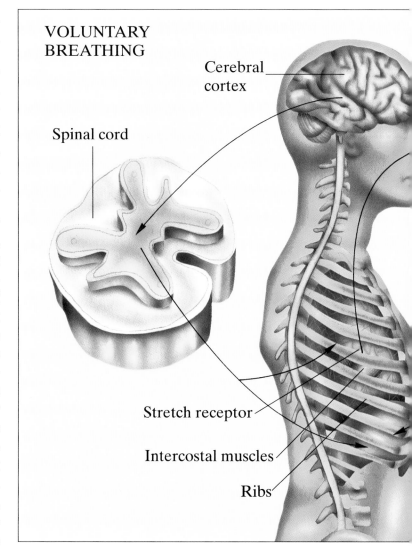

**VOLUNTARY BREATHING**

Cerebral cortex

Spinal cord

Stretch receptor

Intercostal muscles

Ribs

Cerebrum

*o the brain's respiratory centre. Then breathing-in stops. We also control our breathing when we want to, sending the muscles instructions from the cerebral cortex.*

*The medulla oblongata is the lowest part of the brain stem. In it lies the respiratory centre. An excess of carbon dioxide in blood going to the brain causes signals to go to the muscles to speed up breathing.*

▶

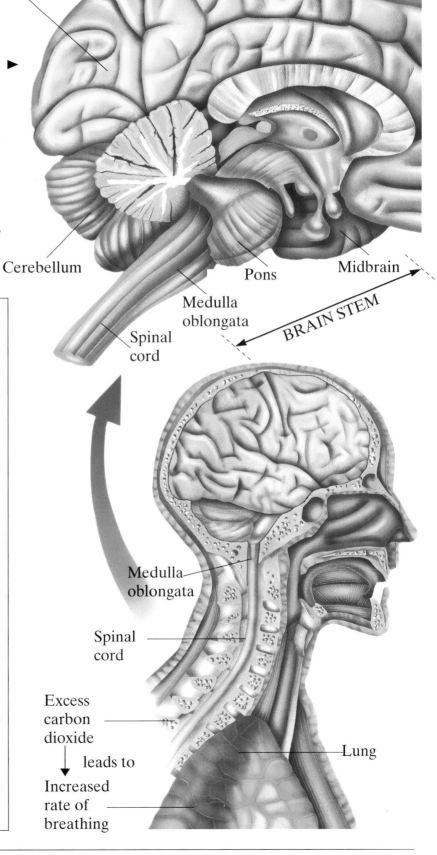

Cerebellum

Pons

Midbrain

Medulla oblongata

BRAIN STEM

Spinal cord

## INVOLUNTARY BREATHING

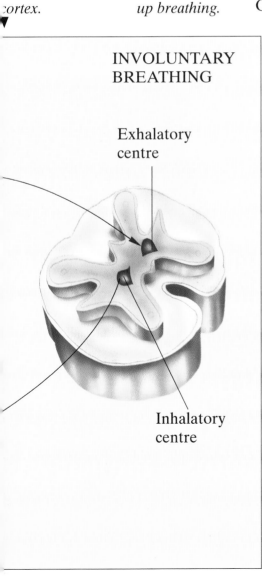

Exhalatory centre

Inhalatory centre

Medulla oblongata

Spinal cord

Excess carbon dioxide

⬇

leads to

Increased rate of breathing

Lung

# Finding out

## Air conditioning

Even on a very dry day, the air we breathe out contains moisture. You can see this when you breathe on a mirror or a sheet of glass. Dry air picks up moisture from the mucous membranes lining our air passages, at the same time as it is warmed to blood temperature; breathe gently through your mouth on to your hand, and your breath feels warm.

## Mouth to mouth

Someone who has stopped breathing will soon suffer permanent brain damage from lack of oxygen. They can sometimes be revived by mouth-to-mouth resuscitation. The person carrying this out pinches the patient's nose to seal the passages, then takes in a deep breath and, placing their mouth completely over that of the patient, breathes into it strongly. The patient's chest will rise as air enters the lungs, and there will be enough oxygen in the breath to keep the patient alive. After a few breaths, the helper pushes firmly on the chest to stimulate the heart. It is a good idea to take first-aid lessons to learn how to do this properly.

## How much air do *you* breathe?

The amount of air each person breathes in and out varies, depending on factors such as their age, sex, size and health. So does the control they have over their breathing. Singers, for example, who are trained to take in deep breaths and let them out slowly, are much more efficient breathers than most people!

Take a watch and ask your friends to take a deep breath and hold it as long as they possibly can. You will find that adults in general, and people of any age who take regular exercise, can hold their breath longer than others. Now ask them to take in a deep breath and count while breathing out. Do the same people do best?

Ask your friends to blow up a balloon each, using all the air they can breathe out in a single breath. Then compare the size of the different balloons.

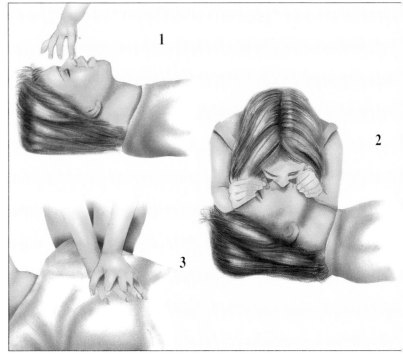

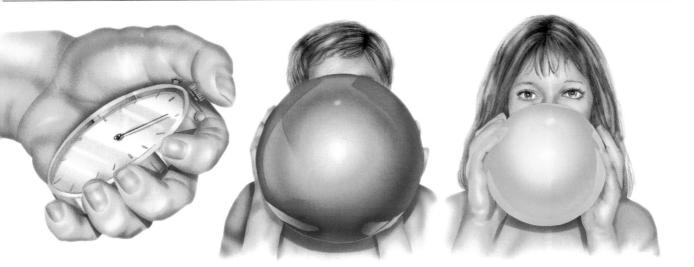

## The longer, the deeper

Men have much deeper voices than women. This is because their vocal cords are longer. See how this works with the strings of a guitar.

When you pluck a guitar string it gives a certain note. If you press the string on to the neck of the instrument, the note it gives will be higher, and it will get higher the closer you move your hand towards the body of the guitar because you are shortening the string.

## What is a resonance chamber?

A guitar and a spare string for it will show you what a difference resonance chambers make to a sound. Tighten the string between two nails on a table, and pluck it. The sound it makes is weak and 'dead'. Now pluck the same size string on a guitar. The sound will be much louder and richer because it resonates in the hollow body of the guitar.

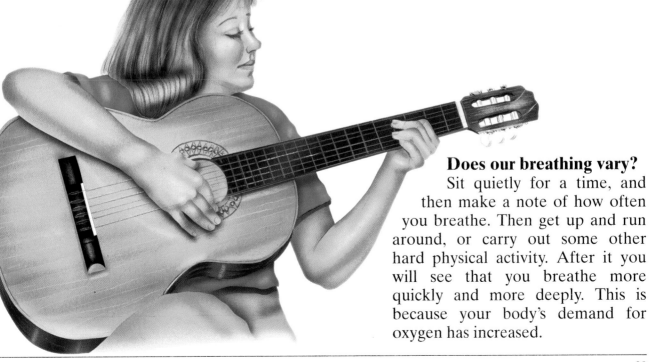

## Does our breathing vary?

Sit quietly for a time, and then make a note of how often you breathe. Then get up and run around, or carry out some other hard physical activity. After it you will see that you breathe more quickly and more deeply. This is because your body's demand for oxygen has increased.

# Index and glossary